D1052797

Presented to

My dearest sister Gloria

On the occasion of

Christmas 2000

From

Suzi

Date

December 17, 2000

©MCMXCIX by Barbour Publishing, Inc.

ISBN 1-57748-586-6

Scripture quotations are taken from the Authorized King James Version of the Bible.

Selections by Sheila Stewart and Donna I. Lange are used with the author's permission.

Published by Barbour Publishing, Inc., P. O. Box 719, Uhrichsville, OH 44683
http://www.barbourbooks.com

Member of the
Evangelical Christian
Publishers Association

Printed in China.

FOREVER SISTERS

Written and compiled by
Ellyn Sanna

BARBOUR
PUBLISHING, INC.

My sister! My sweet sister!
if a name
Dearer and purer were
it should be thine.

LORD BYRON

Big Sisters,
Little Sisters . . .
Someone to
Watch Over Me

Surrounded by Love

As the youngest in my family, I didn't have a baby sister—I had three big sisters. Age-wise, I'm separated from the youngest of them by nine years, so in a sense they were more like a set of mothers to me. My brother, who is closer to me in age, taught me all about sibling rivalry—but my sisters taught me about unconditional love.

My sisters played with me and taught me things. They made me laugh and comforted me when I cried. They made my world feel safe, even while they expanded its horizons.

One of my sisters tells me that when I was little she liked to put her hand on my shoulder, delighted and awed by how tiny my bones were. Through all the hurts that life has dealt me, I know I carry hidden inside me that sense that I am somehow special, loved, cared for.

Because, more than anything, my sisters—those tall, strong young women who surrounded me when I was a child—showed me with their hands and voices and laughter that God loved me.

*W*hen Doren was three years old she informed our parents she had to have a baby sister. A year later I was born. Doren often reminded me I had her to thank for this. Was I supposed to feel grateful, needed, loved? I never quite knew, but I know I believed it was my sister's idea that I come into being. I came into the world, then, Doren's child.

CATHY ARDEN

*T*he Bible says that friends are supposed to love all the time, and that a brother is born for adversity....

But what about a sister? What is a sister born for? My sister was born to be the rock of our family. Even before Mother died and Daddy got old, she was the one we depended on. She was the one who always sent the special cards on my birthday and every other occasion. She was the one who made sure our little brother didn't get left out of the family gatherings.

She was the one who showed me what women of faith look like. She taught me how to live.

She made me proud of our family.

CAROLINE BURNS

7

*M*y sister Emily loved the moors.
Flowers brighter than the rose
bloomed in the blackest
of the heath for her;
out of a sullen hollow in a livid hillside,
her mind could make an Eden.
She found in the bleak solitude many and dear
delights; and not the least and best-loved was liberty.
Liberty was the breath of Emily's nostrils.

CHARLOTTE BRONTË

*It's a great comfort to
have an artistic sister.*

LOUISA MAY ALCOTT

A Sense of Responsibility

I was six when my little sister was born. "Please," I had requested, "let's have a girl this time." After all, one little brother was enough in my opinion. So I was relieved and happy when she actually did turn out to be a girl. And she was so tiny, so helpless looking—I was in awe. I'd asked for her, and now she was here: I supposed that must make her my responsibility in a way.

My parents have a picture that was taken not long after she was born. Her mouth is wide open, her eyes squeezed shut, her face is stretched in a scarlet-faced wail. My brother and I are holding her, smiling lovingly down at her. We seem to be either oblivious to her crying, which really must have been impossible, or else fondly ignoring it. We loved our baby sister, though, and in the photograph our arms are wrapped protectively around her.

I think that word—protective—describes the way I always felt about my sister while we were growing up. I tried to make sure she didn't get hurt playing outside, didn't fall and cut herself on the rocks behind our house. I planned how I would rescue her if our house caught on fire during the night. (I planned on saving the rest of the family, too, but I thought I should rescue my sister first because she was the smallest.) In the evenings, when we came in from playing outside, sometimes she would have streaks of blood on her head and neck from blackfly bites, and I would comb the blood out of her hair and wash the bites. And then when we were a bit older, and we moved to a larger town, I swore I'd kill anyone who hurt her.

Now that she's seventeen, she's become my friend as well as my sister; these days, I feel less like a mother to her. I'm not sure why I ever felt I had to mother her in the first place, since we had a perfectly wonderful mother as it was. Maybe it was just because I loved her so much that I didn't want anything to happen to her. Mom wasn't always there to look after her, so I thought I should be.

I still love her. I still don't want anything to happen to her—but we're hundreds of miles apart now, and I can't check her over every day to make sure there are no streaks of blood. I know, though, God will look after my sister, and He will do a much better job than I could ever think of doing. He'll even do a better job than our parents could.

I guess I was wrong to think I was the one who could and should protect her. But I loved her so much I wanted to try.

SHEILA STEWART

10

Shared
Secrets

A Secret Language

"Girls, it's bedtime," our mother called.

"Okay, Mom," my sister and I chimed in unison.

I stepped onto the hardwood floor, grabbed the oak door frame to balance myself, and leaned against the wall. I flung a paper ball into my sister's bedroom and hurried back into my room. Then I waited for her signal.

Tap, tap, tap. I responded with three quick knocks on the wall that divided our bedrooms.

"Mom, I need to go to the bathroom," I heard my sister say.

"Hurry up," Mom answered

My sister slid down the hallway, a straight shot into the bathroom. After I heard the door close, I got into position. In the corner of my bedroom was a sink, and I stood there now, next to the bathroom wall. I leaned over the white porcelain fixture and grabbed the faucet's two handles. Then I listened.

From the other side of the wall I heard a faucet turn on and off, creating a rhythm like Morse code. I responded: two short turns, one long hard turn. Cold water splashed on my hands as I answered my sister's message.

"Ann, are you in bed?" Mom called to my sister.

"I'm going."

We turned the faucets off and giggled as my sister retreated to her room.

When I heard the radiator hiss, I sneaked out of my bedroom and crawled into my sister's bed. We snuggled like spoons in a drawer and fell asleep.

Although my sister and I are adults now, our secret language is still an important part of our relationship. Communication is vital to all relationships—and if we encourage our children to develop a secret language with each other, perhaps they'll understand how much we all need a secret language with God as well.

Why do we use a secret language? I suppose because we want to participate in each other's lives and help each other. We want to feel needed and secure; we want to know we have a companion in life. Having a special language keeps our relationship unique.

As sisters, developing a secret language is simple. A mispronounced word takes on a coded meaning. A nickname becomes a term of endearment. We spell out our love with secret codes and knocks on the wall. As my sister and I grew older, we used other methods to communicate—telephone calls, letters, and e-mail. We schedule special time to be together—and however we communicate, we still use coded words and secret phrases.

Sometimes we communicate without words. My sister and I both remember a particular phone call during my first semester of college. We said nothing. We just cried. We didn't need to speak to communicate our message: We missed each other. Just as when we snuggled like spoons in a drawer, the message was clear: We were secure and loved.

Our relationship with God is not so very different. He knows us and want us to know Him intimately. He's interested in the big events and the details of our lives. We can communicate in private, anywhere, and we can feel a secret excitement as He answers us. In our relationship with Him, we are secure and loved.

Tonight, I called out the familiar words: "Girls, it's bedtime."

"Okay, Mom," my daughters chimed in unison.

One of them added, "Mom, I need to go to the bathroom."

"Hurry up," I responded.

When I heard the humidifier hum, I walked down the hallway and looked in at an empty bedroom. I turned the corner and entered my other daughter's room. The two sisters were already sound asleep, snuggled like spoons in a drawer.

They already have a secret language with each other. Perhaps they'll also have a secret language with God.

DONNA I. LANGE

14

*Someone Who
Shares
My Memories*

Often, in old age,
they become each other's chosen
and most happy companions.
In addition to their shared memories of childhood
and of their relationship to each other's children,
they share memories of the same home,
the same homemaking style,
and the same small prejudices about housekeeping
that carry the echoes of their mother's voice.

Margaret Mead

A Shared Past

I have many good friends, women who are so close I could almost think of them as sisters. But only my flesh and blood sisters share my past. We have the same set of Christmas memories in our heads, we loved the same childhood pets, and the same collection of fragrances spells home to us. We were raised by the same two parents, and we alone know exactly what that means.

My grandmother used to tell a story about an old woman who was robbed of all her clothing and possessions while she was asleep; when she woke up, she looked at herself and didn't know who she was. Sometimes I feel a little like that old lady. I look around and I can hardly recognize myself. Time has stolen away so much of what I used to think was essential to my identity.

Times like those are when I need my sisters. Even when I'm stout and seventy, they'll remember a little girl in pigtails. They keep my childhood safe inside their heads—and when they look at me, they always know who I am.

*I*s the world all grown up?
Is childhood dead?
Or is there not in the bosom
of the wisest and the best,
some of the child's heart left,
to respond to its earlier enchantments.

CHARLES LAMB

How vast a memory has Love!

ALEXANDER POPE

*G*od gave us memories that we might
have roses in December.

JAMES M. BARRIE

*T*he desire to be and have a sister is a primitive and profound
one that may have everything or
nothing to do with the family
a woman is born to.
It is a desire to know and be known
by someone who shares blood and body,
history and dreams, common ground
and the unknown adventures of the future,
darkest secrets and the glassiest beads of truth.

ELIZABETH FISHEL

*H*eirlooms we don't have in our family.
But stories we've got.

ROSE CHERNIN

*One of
Life's Comforts*

There can be no situation in life
in which the conversation of
my dear sister will not administer
some comfort to me.

LADY MARY WORTLEY MONTAGU

One can bear grief,
but it takes two to be glad.

ELBERT HUBBARD

21

Understanding

Sharing my life with my sister is truly one of the comforts of my life—a little like putting tired, pinched feet into warm, soft slippers. No matter what happens to me, I always know it won't seem quite so bad once I've talked to her. I like her sympathy of course—but even more, I think, I like her belief in who I am. I feel stronger because she takes for granted her confidence in me. Talking with her, the hard things don't seem so hard, and the funny things are even funnier. Together, we find that laughter is hidden everywhere.

When death hit our family, my sister and I stayed up all night, talking and talking until we found the joy even in the darkness. When she had her babies, I fell in love, as awed and delighted as if they were my own. When I was in labor with my own children, I talked with her on the phone and was reassured by her experience. All my life, she's gone ahead to break the path for me; I watch her and learn from her, and I am comforted.

Sometimes when we get together, we laugh until we cry; sometimes we cry until we laugh. Our husbands can only watch us, shaking their heads. But we understand.

And that understanding gives us comfort.

*M*y sister and my sister's child,
Myself and children three,
Will fill the chaise; so you must ride
On horseback after we.

WILLIAM COWPER

*A woman should always
stand by a woman.*

EURIPIDES

A Letter

Salem, January 15, 1767

Dear Sister,

Your kind letter I received today and am greatly rejoiced to [hear] you are all so well. I was uneasy at not hearing from you, indeed my dear sister the winter never seem'd so tedious to me in the world. I daily count the days between this and the time I may probably see you. I could never feel so comfortable as I at present do, if I thought I should spend another winter here. Indeed my sister I cannot bear the thought of staying here so far from all my friends if Mr. Cranch can do as well nigher. I would give a great deal only to know I was within ten miles of you if I could not see you. Our children will never seem so natural to each other as if they liv'd where they could see one another oftener...

MARY SMITH CRANCH
to her sister, Abigail Adams

*Sisters and friends are
God's life preservers.*

ANONYMOUS

*A ministering angel
shall my sister be.*

SHAKESPEARE

A Letter

I thank and bless you my dearest Henrietta and Arabel…my own dearest kindest sisters! What I suffered in reaching Orleans—at last holding all these letters in my hands, can only be measured by my deep gratitude to you, and by the tears and kisses I spent upon every line of what you wrote to me…dearest kindest that you are…

My thoughts cling to you all, and will not leave their hold.

ELIZABETH BARRETT BROWNING
to her sisters

Dear Sister

Yet still my fate permits me this relief,
To write to lovely Delia all my grief.
To you alone I venture to complain;
From others hourly strive to hide my pain.

ABIGAIL COLMAN DENNIE
to her sister

A Sister's Help

*W*hen my family and I went camping, my sister and I would always go to the rest room together before we went to bed. On one evening, we were at a campground that happened to be fairly crowded. I took a shower and brushed my teeth and stood leaning against the wall near the door to wait for Anna to finish with her shower. The bathroom was filled with women who talked and laughed as they clustered around the sinks and mirrors. I noticed that Anna seemed to be taking longer than usual.

Finally she emerged from the shower stall. She was shivering, her lips blue and her teeth chattering.

"How do you turn on the hot water?" she asked me as soon as we left the building. She had taken her whole shower in icy cold water, too embarrassed to ask me for help because of all the other women in the bathroom. To make matters worse, she's allergic to cold. Her body was covered with red, itchy welts.

We laugh about that experience now, remembering it. We

laughed at the time, too, after we got Anna warmed up again. If I had had any idea that she was having trouble, I would have helped her, but I didn't know.

Sisters help each other; I would be willing to help my sister solve much greater problems than shower faucets, just as she would help me. Before we can help each other, though, we have to know there is a problem. If we let other things come between us—like a bathroom full of unknown, noisy women—we might not be able to get the comfort our sisters could give.

Even when I don't think she can do anything about my problems, I still like to talk to Anna about them. Sometimes she really can't do anything, but talking to her still makes me feel better. And sometimes she has a solution I wouldn't have expected, that I would have missed if I hadn't talked to her.

SHEILA STEWART

A Mirror to
Show Me Myself

The Real Me

I can impress my friends. I'm fairly good at keeping my petty flaws well hidden —and I usually keep the not-so-petty ones wrapped up even tighter. I confide in my friends and share my life—but before we meet, I always brush my hair and put on my makeup.

But my sister knows what I look like first thing in the morning. "Ellyn," she sarcastically says, as I come stumbling out of bed, my hair a rat's nest, circles under my eyes, "you're a thing of rare beauty."

I can't fool her very often. When my husband and I argue, my friends always take my side; after all, they usually only hear my carefully edited version of the disagreement. But my sister knows the truth. And she's never afraid to say it.

Sometimes I wish my achievements impressed her a little more. But in the end, I know I value even higher the gift she gives me. She looks at me with her sharp eyes, sees it all—the snarls and baggy eyes and crabby selfish streaks—and she loves me anyway.

When I talk with her, I find I see myself a little clearer—not the dressed-up me I wear in public, but the whole me, the me I take into God's presence. Makeup is fine in its place—but sometimes I need the cold, clean, unconditional grace that washes away all my cosmetics.

What families have in common
the world around is that
they are the place where people learn
who they are and how to be that way.

JEAN ILLSEY CLARKE

A sister is both
your mirror—
and your opposite.

ELIZABETH FISHEL

Unconditional Acceptance

When my little sister was in her early teens, she suddenly decided that the family would be better off without her. After all, didn't the perfect family consist of two children, a girl and a boy? We didn't need her. My brother and I got along so well, she was just in the way.

"Of course, we like you," my brother and I told her over and over again. "We think you're great. We love you. Our family would be boring without you." But she thought we were just trying to make her feel better.

She's seventeen now and not quite as skeptical about our feelings for her. Part of the problem these days, though, is that my brother and I live away from home, much closer to each other than to her. It's hard for her to be left behind when she would really like to see us more often. I wrote to her a little while ago, just wanting to tell her how much I enjoy talking to her on the phone as well as spending time with her when we get a chance to visit each other. She thought the card was wonderful. She always seems surprised when I tell her things like that.

Sometimes I feel the same way with God. Why would He like me anyhow? Acceptance, the thing we long for, is sometimes so hard for us to believe we have actually gained. As sisters, we help each other grasp the amazing fact: Someone not only puts up with us, she loves us; she enjoys be-ing with us, and she would find life incomplete without us. From this point, we stretch to reach the next stepping stone: God sees us as infinitely valuable. He loves us; He created us because He didn't want to be without us. Through Christ, we have God's unconditional acceptance.

SHEILA STEWART

*Y*ea, I have loved thee
with an everlasting love:
therefore with lovingkindness
have I drawn thee.

JEREMIAH 31:3

A Friend
Forever

No Friend Like a Sister

For there is no friend like a sister,
In calm or stormy weather,
To cheer one on the tedious way,
To fetch one if one goes astray,
To lift one if one totters down,
To strengthen whilst one stands.

CHRISTINA ROSSETTI

A true sister is a friend who listens with her heart.

ANONYMOUS

The greatest gift we can give one another is
rapt attention to one another's existence.

SUE ATCHLEY EBAUGH

My Sister, My Friend

Somewhere along the way, my big sister became one of my closest friends. I'm not sure when it happened. It might have been years ago when she stayed up late talking to me after my first boyfriend broke up with me. Maybe it was when we realized we liked the same books, and started saying to each other all the time, "Have you read...?" or "You should read..." It might have been the time she caught me crying after my first day of work; she poured me a glass of ice tea, listened to me talk, and helped me face another day. Or it could have been the afternoon when we she and I held my grandmother until she died. And it might have been just some small ordinary moment when we both thought something silly was funny—like the time my sisters and I tried out a water bed together and laughed until we cried.

All I know is this—all those moments of love and understanding and laughter add up to a friendship I'll never lose. The fact that we're also tied by blood just makes our friendship stronger.

*T*here's a special kind
of freedom sisters enjoy.
Freedom to share
innermost thoughts,
to ask a favor,
to show their true feelings.
The freedom to simply be themselves.

ANONYMOUS

In thee my soul shall own combined
The sister and the friend.

CATHERINE KILLIGREW

*S*isters is probably the most
competitive relationship within the family,
but once the sisters are grown,
it becomes the strongest relationship.

MARGARET MEAD

38

To My Sister

*M*y sister! 'tis a wish of mine)
Now that the morning meal is done,
Make haste, your morning task resign;
Come forth and feel the sun.

One moment now may give us more
Than years of toiling reason;
Our minds shall drink at every pore
The spirit of the season.

Then come, my sister! Come I pray
With speed put on your woodland dress;
And bring no book: for this one day
We'll give to idleness.

WILLIAM WORDSWORTH

Sisterhood is
a powerful thing.

ROBIN MORGAN

*A sister is a gift of God,
sent from above to
make life worthwhile here below.*

ANONYMOUS

A perfect sister I am not,
But I'm thankful for the one I've got.

ANONYMOUS

40